DORSET'S LEGACY
IN PUBLIC STATUES

Michael Russell Wood

Aley

First published in 2017 by John Aley, Bridport, Dorset.

ISBN 978-0-9526329-5-5

© Michael Russell Wood 2017

British Library Cataloguing in Publication Data.
A catalogue record for this book is available from
the British Library.

All photographs by the author, except where credited otherwise.

Design: Luke Murray

Printed by The Dampier Press, Sherborne, Dorset

Contents

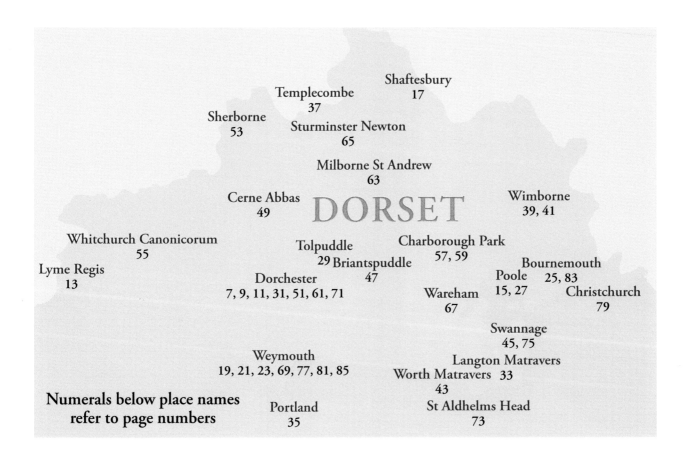

DORSET'S LEGACY IN PUBLIC STATUES

Shaftesbury
17

Templecombe
37

Sherborne
53

Sturminster Newton
65

Milborne St Andrew
63

Cerne Abbas
49

DORSET

Wimborne
39, 41

Whitchurch Canonicorum
55

Tolpuddle
29 Briantspuddle
47

Charborough Park
57, 59

Lyme Regis
13

Dorchester
7, 9, 11, 31, 51, 61, 71

Bournemouth
Poole   25, 83
15, 27

Wareham
67

Christchurch
79

Swannage
45, 75

**Numerals below place names
refer to page numbers**

Weymouth
19, 21, 23, 69, 77, 81, 85

Langton Matravers
Worth Matravers   33
43

Portland
35

St Aldhelms Head
73

Introduction

WHEN I DECIDED to produce another book in the 'Dorset's Legacy' series, it seemed that a volume about statues in Dorset would be an interesting subject to investigate, and so it has proved.

I have not been able to include every sculpture on public display, but all those that are in this book have an interesting or bizarre story to tell. The majority of the sculptures are figurative but I have included some other works for their particular interest.

Nearly all the statues I found in Dorset were created from just before the turn of the 19th century to the present day. Several statues were created to honour the memory of people who were much admired after their death, but others were made while the subject was still alive in order to thank or flatter them. George III and Sir Henry Edwards, both in Weymouth, are good examples of statues made during the lifetime of the subject.

Most memorial statues are cast in bronze while those marking places such as Portland and Langton Matravers are chiselled from the stone of the area. Many of the animal sculptures, except the Dray Horse in Dorchester, are made from composite ingredients that can be worked relatively easily by the sculptor but are strong and weather resistant.

There has been an upsurge during the last twenty years in the commissioning and installation of statues. In 2016 alone, two important figurative works were unveiled; Sir George Somers in Lyme Regis and H.M. The Queen Mother in Poundbury. The millennium was marked by several works being commissioned, including The Dorset Shepherd in Durngate Street, Dorchester, The Stone Mason in Langton Matravers, The Spirit of Portland and the Skateboarder in the Library Garden in Wimborne.

We may not have as many statues on public display in Dorset as some counties, but those we have are worth keeping and cherishing.

"Time, which antiquates antiquities and hath an art to make dust of all things, hath yet spared these minor monuments." *Sir Thomas Browne (1605-1682)*

Michael Russell Wood   **Spring 2017**

1

Sculpture Creation

ONE DEFINITION of sculpture is 'the art of making three dimensional figurative or abstract forms'; another, 'the articulation of volume and mass in space'. However, in this book we are mainly concerned with figurative sculpture.

The two basic techniques are the subtractive and the additive methods. In the first of these, the artist usually starts with a block of wood or stone, carving or chipping away until the desired form is achieved. A fine example of this is the Spirit of Portland (page 35), hand carved with chisel and mallet from a large piece of Portland stone. Another, at Langton Matravers, is the Stonemason (page 33), carved from Purbeck stone.

Carving is a high risk technique since one slip of the chisel could result in the ruination of the whole piece. Noses and other extremities are particularly vulnerable, damage to which can result in many hours of highly skilled remedial work.

The additive method offers more scope for alteration and modification since, as the name implies, the artwork is built up from scratch. The sculptor can choose modelling clay, direct wax or any malleable material from which a mould can be made and a cast taken. This is usually done in plaster for keeping as a copy, in wax for casting into bronze using the lost wax method, or using a specialist concrete which can also be used to build a sculpture from scratch, usually around an inner armature.

An early 1800's material called Coade Stone, or Lithodipyra, was used to create the sculpture of George III (page 19). Animals, such as the deer (page 57) were also constructed employing this method, which was preceded by the production of working maquettes or small scale adjustable versions.

Most public sculptures are cast in bronze, an alloy comprising 90% copper and 10% tin, using the lost wax method, a technique first used around 3700 BC. The sculptor will start by modelling the piece on a small scale, so the sculptor and the person commissioning the work can modify or alter the piece without difficulty or much expense.

Once approved, the sculptor will make the full size version from which a plaster piece mould or a flexible gel mould (kept in shape with an outer casing of plaster or fibreglass) is made. Usually a plaster master will be taken from this mould to preserve the artwork.

Wax is then poured into the mould to the thickness required for the bronze. When necessary, a core material of brick dust and plaster is poured into the void, held in place by cut nails or metal pins. The cooled wax positive is then coated in a material similar to that of the core and placed in a kiln to melt and burn out the wax positive. The molten bronze at 1,200°C is then poured into the void created by the lost wax.

Although this immensely skilled and elaborate method is still used in modern fine art foundries, a system called colloidal silica or ceramic shell casting is now commonly used for precision hot metal casting, where the wax is coated with heat resistant silica slurry which, when cured, will also be placed in a kiln in order to melt out the wax. Whilst still hot the mould is removed from the kiln and molten bronze is poured into it.

Most large sculptures, such as the Dray Horse (page 61), are cast in several pieces and then skillfully welded together so they appear to be made from one piece of bronze. After cooling any moulding marks are removed and the statue is treated with a corrosive solution to produce the required patina.

Some artists use sheet metal that is cut, bent and welded, a good example of which is King Alfred the Great (page 17). It is a very imposing statue, but unlikely to last as long as those made of bronze. The main threat to bronze statues is their value to unscrupulous scrap metal dealers. As recently as 2007 several life-size bronzes by John Waddell were stolen for the value of the metal.

Other materials of which statues are made include the plastic Wenlock (page 81) and, of course, the ephemeral sand sculptures of Weymouth (page 85).

2

Commemorative Statues

WILLIAM BARNES, who wrote many gentle poems in the Dorset dialect, is commemorated by this fine statue that stands outside St Peter's church in High West Street, Dorchester. It was sculpted by Roscoe Mullins, paid for by 90 good people of Dorchester and erected in 1889.

Barnes, who lived from 1801 to 1886, as well as being a poet and linguist, was a tireless educator and rector of Winterborne Came from 1862 until his death. He was a man of great stamina, walking many miles every day visiting his parishioners. In a snowy February, at the age of 80, he was known to have walked 15 miles and taken services for a wedding, a funeral and an office for the sick all on the same day.

This is a man who truly deserved to be commemorated and is an example of strength of character and rectitude to us all.

WILLIAM BARNES

1801. — 1886.

ZOO NOW I HOPE HIS KINDLY FEÄCE
IS GONE TO VIND A BETTER PLEÄCE
BUT STILL WI' VO'K A-LEFT BEHIND
HE'LL ALWAYS BE A-KEPT IN MIND.

This statue of Thomas Hardy stands at the Top O' Town, Dorchester, remembering Dorset's most famous and loved author and poet. Born in 1840, apart from five years in London, he lived all his life in Dorset dying in 1928 at Max Gate, his home in Dorchester.

Up to the age of 27, he had been carrying on his original profession of architect, but when he returned to Dorset, ill health having forced him to leave London, he became a full time writer. Over the years he wrote many novels including Tess of the d'Urbervilles, Far from the Madding Crowd and Jude the Obscure as well as publishing numerous poems. He liked to think of himself as a poet first and author second.

Eric Kennington, probably the most famous and talented sculptor at the time, created this image of Thomas Hardy. It was unveiled on 2nd September 1931 by J.M. Barrie, author of Peter Pan, who was a close friend of Hardy.

Various ideas have been mooted for moving the statue to another part of Dorchester, but this is unlikely to happen, leaving Hardy happy in his existing position.

27th October 2016 was an important day in Poundbury, Prince Charles' Dorchester village or, as some call it, Prince Charles' Dorchester suburb, when Her Majesty the Queen unveiled the statue of her mother. The Royal Party included Prince Philip, Prince Charles and Camilla, Duchess of Cornwall, who arrived in Dorchester by train and proceeded to Queen Mother Square to perform the ceremony.

Created by respected artist Philip Jackson, the bronze statue depicts the Queen Mother when she was 51 and just widowed. It is larger than life size and is the same as her statue in the Mall in London.

The Queen Mother lived a long life of public service, dying at the age of 102. She was an icon of indomitable spirit during World War II and had supported her husband throughout his life, especially when he unexpectedly became king after his brother abdicated. She gave much support and advice to Prince Charles who called her 'my darling grandmother'. This magnificent statue makes an excellent centrepiece for the wide open space of Queen Mother Square.

Sir George Somers stands in the Langmoor Gardens, Lyme Regis, looking out over the harbour and sea. He was born in Lyme Regis in 1554 and by the time he was 33 he was a captain in the Royal Navy capturing several Spanish ships and consequently amassing considerable wealth from the prize money.

He continued serving in the Royal Navy and in 1603 he was knighted. He represented Lyme Regis in Parliament and was also mayor of the town. Like Patrick O'Brian's Jack Aubrey he was described as 'a lion at sea and a lamb on land'. In 1609 Somers led a fleet of seven vessels in his flagship 'Sea Venture', taking pioneers and relief supplies to a settlement in Virginia. A terrible storm hit the little fleet in mid-Atlantic, Somers being wrecked on what was to become Bermuda. He claimed the island for Britain and eventually died there having founded the colony.

This statue was unveiled on 26th July 2016 marking the twinning of Lyme Regis with St Georges, Bermuda.

The sculptor, Ron Mole, has truly captured the strong character of Somers and this statue will help perpetuate the links between Lyme Regis and Bermuda.

ADMIRAL
SIR GEORGE SOMERS KT
1554 — 1610
FOUNDER OF BERMUDA

THIS STATUE IS DONATED TO THE TOWN OF LYME REGIS
BY CHAIRMAN BJ M°HARDY AND THE MEMBERS OF
THE LYME REGIS ST GEORGES TWINNING ASSOCIATION
AND DONATIONS FROM MANY OTHERS

On Poole quay sits the figure of Lord Baden-Powell waiting to take a party of Boy Scouts or Girl Guides to Brownsea Island for a camp.

This statue, created by Scottish artist David Annand, was commissioned and inspired by the efforts of Brian Woolgar to mark the centenary of the Scouting and Girl Guides movements.

Although Lord Baden-Powell's name is chiefly associated with the Scouting Movement he had a distinguished military career in the British army, serving from 1876 to 1910 in India and Africa. During the second Boer War in 1899, he successfully defended the town of Mafeking, being promoted to the rank of Major General before leaving the army.

The Scouting Movement continues to flourish, teaching boys and girls about many things but mainly the good upright values of honesty and self-reliance.

Alfred the Great surveys the garden of the Abbey at Shaftesbury and the country towards South Dorset.

He was sculpted in the early 1990's by Andrew Du Mont and unveiled in 1994 on his original site at King Alfred's Middle School. During a reorganisation of the schools in Shaftesbury in 2004, King Alfred's Middle School disappeared and the statue was moved to the Abbey Gardens.

Made from sheet metal that was cut, folded, shaped and welded by the sculptor, the statue, makes a very impressive presence dominating the peaceful Abbey Garden.

Alfred really was a truly great man – frustrating Viking assaults on his kingdom of Wessex that he governed from 871 to 899. He was a highly intelligent king who, as well as being a natural leader, did his best to improve life in Wessex for all his people by education, well balanced laws and maintaining the peace. One of his daughters, Æthelgifu, became Abbess of Shaftesbury, so it is appropriate for him to be commemorated here by this statue.

King George III visited and stayed in Weymouth 14 times from 1789 onwards. These visits gained much kudos for Weymouth and King George must have enjoyed the town since it probably helped relieve his porphyria. The citizens of Weymouth were of course delighted by these visits; the whole court would descend on the town and the increase in trade was enormous.

Made of Coade stone, or Lithodipyra, the statue was originally mooted in 1802 and designed by the architect James Hamilton. The statue was soon ready but the king fell ill and the project was locked away. In 1809, to celebrate the fiftieth year of King George's reign, the statue was placed in position at the junction of St Mary Street and St Thomas Street on a magnificent plinth where it stands to this day.

In 2007, after years of neglect, the Weymouth and Portland Borough Council had the statue restored. This work was paid for by The Heritage Lottery Fund.

Twenty layers of old paintwork were removed and replaced with fresh paint and gold leaf, the supporting metalwork also being replaced with stainless steel. So King George III can continue in all his splendour to look down on the people of Weymouth for years to come.

There are over 60 statues of Queen Victoria in the United Kingdom and this one is at the end of the Esplanade in Weymouth, opposite St John's Church. She is looking south whereas George III, at the other end of the Esplanade, is looking north.

The sculptor of this bronze statue is unknown but it was sponsored by The Mayor of Weymouth, John Bragg and the Town Clerk Richard Nicholas Howard and it was paid for by public subscription to commemorate the life of Queen Victoria who had just died.

It was unveiled by HRH Princess Beatrice (Princess Henry of Battenberg), Victoria's youngest daughter, on 20th October 1902.

Queen Victoria reigned for 63 years, dying on 22nd January 1901. During this period of widespread changes in all aspects of British life from industry to empire building, scientific research and cultural change, she was a strong influence for strict moral views and universally admired for setting the highest standards of moral probity.

The third statue on the sea front at Weymouth is that of Sir Henry Edwards, which stands by the Alexandra Gardens. He was the member of parliament for Weymouth and Melcombe Regis from 1867 to 1885 when it ceased to be a parliamentary borough.

This statue was erected in 1886, paid for by public subscription 'to perpetuate the memory of the public services and munificent charity and private worth' of Sir Henry Edwards. He did not die till 1897 so he was honoured with this statue during his lifetime.

He was very beneficent to the town. Ten cottage homes or alms houses on Boot Hill known as Edwards Avenue, as well as Edwardsville in Rodwell Avenue, a home for elderly locals, were all built and richly endowed by him. They are today run by Weymouth Town Charities. He also provided an annual dinner for the old people of the town to say nothing of building new premises for the Working Men's Club in Mitchell Street.

Here was a man who truly deserved a statue to acknowledge the good that he had done.

The Bournemouth International Centre, known as the BIC, is a popular venue for political party conferences as well as concerts, but just near the entrance stands a remarkable and humorous statue commemorating two of the founders of Bournemouth.

In 1999 the Mayor and Mayoress of Bournemouth, Keith and Eileen Rawlings, at no public cost, commissioned Corfe-based sculptor Jonathan Sells to create a work; the subjects chosen were Lewis Tregonwell and Christopher Creeke.

Tregonwell, a wealthy man, had been a captain in the Dorset Rangers Coastal Division in 1803, living at Winterborne Anderson. His wife Henrietta took a fancy to the Bournemouth area and by 1812 he had built a grand house, Bourne Cliff. Tregonwell built several small houses in the area as well as planting many conifers that later attracted people to the area; their tang and the warm salty breezes, made it an ideal place for convalescence. He later leased his house to the Marchioness of Exeter which, after many modifications, is now The Royal Exeter Hotel.

Christopher Creeke was appointed Town Surveyor and Inspector of Nuisances in 1856 and it is he who designed the basic layout of the town with curved roads that were suitable for the large houses at the time. He is portrayed sitting on the lavatory and Tregonwell has a bucket and spade under his arm.

The statue has a serious side as well. It commemorates the three Bournemouth holders of the Victoria Cross - Corporal Noble, Sergeant Riggs and Lieutenant Seagrim.

This large work is outside the Royal National Lifeboat Institution's headquarters in West Quay Road, Poole. It depicts a lifeboat crewman rescuing a drowning person from a rough sea.

Designed by Sam Holland, it is a permanent memorial to all the lifeboat crewmen who have died selflessly rescuing shipwrecked sailors and others from the sea.

Unveiled on Thursday, 3rd September 2009, the names of those who lost their lives rescuing others are listed together with the motto of Sir William Hillary: 'With courage nothing is impossible.' It reminds us that there are men and women who voluntarily carry out acts of heroism and bravery without a thought for their own safety, and it restores our faith in human nature.

The Royal National Lifeboat Institution is a charity devoted solely to saving lives at sea and is funded entirely by voluntary contributions with no government funding whatsoever. Not only does it operate lifeboats for use in offshore waters it also operates inshore rigid inflatables that rescue many seaside visitors who get into difficulties caused by wind, tide or ignorance.

Anyone wishing to contribute to the work of the Royal National Lifeboat Institution should contact their nearest lifeboat station or the RNLI Headquarters at West Quay Road, Poole, Dorset.

This statue is in front of the Tolpuddle Martyrs' Museum. It depicts George Loveless, the leader of the Tolpuddle Martyrs, languishing in Dorchester prison recovering from sickness before being deported to Australia with the other martyrs.

This statue was commissioned by the Public and Commercial Services Union and executed by the sculptor Thompson Dagnal in 2000. The uprights at the back of the piece were shaped by students at Weymouth College, each one representing one of the martyrs. On the back of the uprights are carved the words spoken by George Loveless at his trial – "We will, we will, we will be free".

In the early 1830's conditions for farm labourers were extremely hard with farmers only willing to pay nine shillings per week or less. This was a sub-poverty amount and with George Loveless, who was also a Methodist lay preacher, a perfectly legal friendly society was formed to try to improve the labourers' conditions. The employers rejected any requests for a better wage and the six men were arrested and charged, under an obscure law, prohibiting secret oaths. They were found guilty at Dorchester Assizes and ordered to be deported to New South Wales.

Meanwhile a campaign for their release was led by Lord John Russell who secured their pardon and return to England. One of the men stayed in Tolpuddle the others eventually found new lives in Canada.

The bravery and fearless belief in liberty of these men, particularly George Loveless, inspired the start of trade unions in England.

3

Figures

THE DORSET SHEPHERD stands with his dog at his feet in Durngate Street, Dorchester, as if surveying his flock.

At the time of the millennium Tony Kennet, managing director of Henry Ling Ltd. (printers), realised that Dorchester did not have much street art. He commissioned a work from the sculptor John Doubleday, inspired by the William Barnes poem The Shepherd O' The Farm that epitomises Dorset rural life in the late nineteenth century.

Durngate Street was chosen as the site for the Dorset Shepherd since it had strong connections with William Barnes. This was the place where he opened a school in 1835.

Other historical links are the origins of the late lamented brewers Eldridge Pope at the Green Dragon in the same street. Messrs Henry Ling Ltd. should be congratulated for commissioning and donating this sculpture to the town.

An' I do bide all day among
The bleaten sheep, an' pitch their vwold;
An' when the evenen sheades be long
Do zee all a-penn'd an' twold.

from THE SHEPHERD O' THE FARM by William Barnes

This sculpture, The Dorset Shepherd, is a tribute to the quiet heroism and wisdom of pastoralists and cultivators who provide inspiration for the literary tradition associated with Dorchester. It was commissioned to mark the year 2000 by Henry Ling Limited, printers in Dorchester since 1804.   Sculptor: John Doubleday

This statue of a quarryman stands in the churchyard at Langton Matravers. It was created by 87-year-old Mary Spencer Watson to mark one thousand years of quarrying and stone working in Purbeck.

Mary Spencer Watson, who died in 2006, had been a sculptor all her life working very much in the style of the medieval worker carvers. She carved and chiselled her works from a simple block of stone usually Purbeck.

Coming from an artistic family, her father, George Spencer Watson, had been a distinguished portrait painter and Royal Academician. He bought nearby Dunshay Manor in 1923.

Mary lived at Dunshay throughout her life, and during World War II taught in local schools while still creating sculptures from Purbeck stone.

This sculpture is called The Spirit of Portland and it stands beside the road at Priory Corner on the main road from Underhill to Tophill.

The sculptress, Joanna Szuwalska, through her depiction of a stonemason and a fisherman, encapsulates the twin strengths of Portland. The tough resilience of the fisherman and the determination of the stonemason are beautifully captured in this work.

Hewn from a single block of Portland stone, it stands where the Merchant's Railway used to carry blocks of Portland stone down to the dock at Castletown, there to be loaded onto vessels to be shipped all over the world.

The statue was commissioned by Weymouth and Portland Borough Council and was officially unveiled on 18th August 2000, celebrating the millennium.

Templecombe station is just over the border into Somerset but it has this interesting statue standing by the platform.

It was originally commissioned by British Rail for their exhibit at the National Garden Festival at Gateshead, the theme of which was Railway Time. This statue by Siobhan Coppinger and Alec Peever has a railman holding a timetable.

Originally the statue was a sundial with the statue's forearm being the gnomon and fallen pages torn from the timetable being the hours. Ironically, the pages which were sculpted from limestone have disappeared but the main part of the piece cast in bronze is still there. How and why the sculpture migrated from the Garden Festival to Templecombe station is a mystery.

Templecombe was once an important junction for the mainline from the West to London and the Somerset and Dorset railway. With the demise of the Somerset and Dorset Railway in 1965, the station was closed but re-opened in 1983 and since that time it has been gradually refurbished and improved, winning awards for the best-kept small station.

This figure of a Grenadier Guardsman is on the outside of the bell tower of the Minster at Wimborne.

He is known as the Quarter Jack since he strikes every quarter of an hour on the bells with his hammers. He is driven by the works of the astronomical clock that is inside the bell tower.

The astronomical clock face is in the baptistry and shows the sun going round the earth, marking the time on a 24 hour dial as well as the phases of the moon.

The clock dates from the late 1300's but was rebuilt in 1743 and is still going strong. An excellent working model can be seen inside the Minster.

This skateboarder, full of energy and the enthusiasm of youth, is in the garden of the Wimborne Library.

West Dorset sculptress Greta Berlin created this work and exhibited it at a local biennial sculpture and art exhibition, where it was noticed by members of the East Dorset Heritage Trust. They felt it was an ideal work to help celebrate the millennium and so, in due course, it came to stand where it is now.

Greta Berlin was inspired to create this and other sculptures of skateboarders when visiting London. She had noticed, on the South Bank, high culture on the top level and skateboarders enjoying themselves on ground level. It seemed a natural thing for her to do uniting the two cultures with her style of work.

These two pieces are outside the Square and Compasses at Worth Matravers. They are typical examples of local stone worked by quarrymen/carvers.

There is a small museum connected to the inn displaying the different types of Purbeck stone and marble as well as local fossils and other coastal curiosities.

This tavern always has an excellent selection of beers and ciders on draught and a very simple food menu – meat pasty or vegetarian pasty!

The front of Swanage Town Hall seems incongruous in this seaside town, but the elaborate sculpted façade was once part of the Mercer's Hall on Cheapside, London.

Designed in 1670 by Edward Jerman, a pupil of Sir Christopher Wren, it is the emblem of the Mercers' Company, depicting the Virgin Mary in the middle of the sculpture with a cherub on each side.

This piece of London and many other features in Swanage are due to one man, George Burt. The son of a local quarryman, he left to join the contracting firm of his uncle John Mowlem in London, eventually rising to become a partner. Becoming a wealthy man, Burt used some of his fortune to benefit his old home town, utilising many items from the firm's work in London that would otherwise have been scrapped.

Burt built the town hall in 1882/3 and it has been the centre of civic activities in Swanage ever since. Over the years it has been used for many types of meeting, and the council chamber is still in use although the magistrates court is no longer held there.

4

Religious

THESE TWO EFFIGIES are on the war memorial in Briantspuddle. This obelisk, created by Eric Gill just after the Armistice in 1918, remembers those local men who died fighting in World War I.

Best known for his calligraphy, the purity of this memorial shows the width of Gill's vision. He is reputed to have brought this work on a horse and cart from his studio in South-East England to Dorset, subsisting on ham, bread and cider.

With designs by Eric Gill's brother, Leslie MacDonald Gill, in the Arts and Crafts style, Briantspuddle was made into a 'model village' by Sir Ernest Debenham, the London department store owner.

Sir Ernest bought the estate in 1914, wishing to improve the lot of local farmers and improve farming practices. He built cottages for his farm workers that were warm and dry with modern toilet facilities. After his death in 1952 the estate was broken up and sold.

Above the west door of the church of St Mary the Virgin at Cerne Abbas is a medieval stone statue. In a protected niche it depicts the Madonna and Child in a traditional pose.

Fortunately, this was one of the very few similar statues to avoid destruction at the time of the dissolution of the monasteries ordered by King Henry VIII. The Abbey of Cerne was founded in AD 987 but the church was built by the monks for the use of the villagers in the early 1300's.

Cerne Abbas became a prosperous market town that was noted for the quality of the beer brewed here due to the excellent water.

The prosperity of the village diminished rapidly when it was bypassed by the railway. The Cerne Abbas brewery now produces excellent beers in the shadow of the famous Cerne Abbas Giant.

The Chideock Martyrs memorial stands at the eastern end of South Walks, the area once known as Gallows Hill, in Dorchester.

This remarkable group by the celebrated sculptress Dame Elisabeth Frink was installed in 1986 having been funded by numerous individuals, groups of all types and denominations, as well as South West Arts and the Arts Council of Great Britain.

It marks the place where the gallows used to stand and shows two of the Chideock Martyrs in front of the hangman. They had been sentenced to death for the crime of adhering to the Roman Catholic faith, and this group of statues symbolises all the hundreds of people who were persecuted for their religious beliefs during the late 16th and early 17th centuries.

Executions were particularly brutal at this time. The prisoner, having been suspended by his neck, would be butchered while still alive, the heart being removed and then the body dismembered. The head would often be displayed as well as the dismembered body, in prominent places such as gateways and on posts as a warning to anyone who might offend against the laws of the time.

St Aldhelm stands in a niche on the front of The Digby Memorial Church Hall, Sherborne, that was built in 1910 as a memorial to John Kenelm Wingfield Digby who died in 1904.

Below the niche, the shield-of-arms of Sherborne Abbey is held by Mark Parsons, a local butcher and churchwarden. At the time, a master at Sherborne School described the statue 'as one of the very worst specimens of cheap modern Gothic extant'.

St Aldhelm, who died in AD 709, was a scholar who built churches and schools and established the Benedictine monastic order in Malmesbury. He was favoured by King Ine of Wessex who divided the diocese of Wessex in two and Aldhelm was made bishop of Sherborne.

He was also famous as a writer, one of his noted works being De Virginitate (About Virginity) written for the Abbess and nuns of Barking. When he was Abbot of Malmesbury he would often stand in the icy waters of the nearby stream in order to subdue the desires of the flesh.

The church in Whitchurch Canonicorum is dedicated to St Candida and The Holy Cross, but is locally known as The Cathedral of the Vale.

St Wite, whose statue gazes out at us from a niche in the tower wall, was the early name of St Candida. She is famous for her healing powers, particularly for eyesight, and the water from her spring, about a mile to the south, is noted for being beneficial.

Her relics are still in the church in a stone coffin with large holes in the side into which supplicants and pilgrims can pass their diseased limbs for healing or put cloths that could then be put on the affected part of the body. The actual relics are in a lead coffin inside the stone one.

If you visit this magnificent church, search on the west side of the graveyard and you will find the final resting place of Georgi Markov, the Bulgarian author and defector who worked for the BBC and was murdered, probably by the Bulgarian secret police with KGB assistance. On 7th September 1978, as he waited for a bus near Waterloo Bridge, he was stabbed in the back of his leg with an umbrella, whose tip injected a pellet that was loaded with the poison ricin. He died four days later in St James Hospital, Balham, there being no known antidote for this poison.

5

Animals

AS YOU DRIVE along the A31 from Bere Regis towards Wimborne you see the brick wall that encloses the north side of Charborough Park, the home of the Drax family for over 400 years.

The stag which surmounts this entrance arch, no longer used, can appear from some directions, to have five legs. The popular myth is that after the wall and entrance arches had been built in the 1840's by John Sawbridge Drax, he looked from his bedroom window and complained that the stag appeared to have only three legs. This was remedied by adding another one so that the stag seemed to be normally endowed with limbs when viewed from the house.

Sadly this piece of folklore is probably false and the fifth leg was added to support the statue that had become unstable. The fifth leg really looks more like a tree stump against which the deer is rubbing itself.

A short distance further along the A31 towards Wimborne is another identical arch over the main northern entrance to Charborough Park, but this one is surmounted by a lion soutant sculpted from stone.

The lion has always symbolised bravery and stateliness. This sculpture was probably created around the same time that John Sawbridge Drax was elected as Member of Parliament for Wareham, a seat he held, on and off, for nearly 40 years. His direct descendant Richard Drax is now Member of Parliament for South Dorset so there is a long tradition of public service in the Drax family.

John Sawbridge Drax did not have any parliamentary speeches recorded in Hansard, but he may have spoken frequently, since popular belief is that after one of his outbursts, the speaker of the House of Commons ordered the windows to be opened to let out all the hot air. Richard Drax already has over 60 speeches recorded in Hansard, and he is working hard for his constituents and for the good of the country.

As a footnote, there are over two million bricks in the wall alongside the road, so the estate bricklayer has to work hard to keep this Dorset landmark in good order.

This magnificent statue of a dray horse stands where the main entrance to the now defunct Eldridge Pope brewery in Dorchester used to be.

The artist Shirley Pace modelled the sculpture on Drummer, the last dray horse to have worked at the brewery. On 19th April 2014, the piece was paraded through the town, loaded on a cart drawn by two horses before being sited outside the cinema in Brewery Square. He stands 16 feet tall and weighs an impressive one and a half tons. The statue gives off an aura of power and gentleness and expresses the close relationship that man has always had with the horse in peacetime and wartime for both work and pleasure.

Dray horses were used to haul beer to all the Eldridge Pope inns until they were displaced by the motor lorry. Youngs Brewery in London still use some horse drawn drays for deliveries it being both cost effective and excellent advertising.

This graceful stag stands on the flat roof that is part of a house in Milborne St Andrew, adjacent to the A354 road that leads to Blandford from Puddletown.

How the stag arrived at its present location has proved to be a mystery, but is reputed to have been given to a Mr J. Cole by a member of the Drax family in gratitude for his support in an election, probably between 1840 and 1880 when John Sawbridge Drax represented Wareham in the House of Commons.

The stag is noted for being a mediaeval symbol for Christ, stamping on snakes which are symbols of the devil. Pagan folklore, meanwhile, considers the stag to be a woodland deity with the antlers strongly associated with fertility. But the stag is really a symbol of the hunt and country life.

This elegant statue, unnoticed by motorists as they pass through the village, maintains an alert presence looking up the valley towards Milton Abbas.

The Red Lion Inn was a public house on the edge of Sturminster Newton on the A357 road towards Lydlinch and Stalbridge. The inn was closed by the brewers Hall and Woodhouse in the mid 1990's.

It is now a private dwelling but the pub sign, a red lion couchant, still keeps guard over the front door.

Life-size, the black bear statue stands proudly upright on the balcony over the entrance, welcoming guests to The Black Bear Hotel in South Street, Wareham. The building, built in 1722, is listed Grade II, the statue probably being slightly later.

In November 1980, the black bear suddenly changed its colour to yellow. Luckily, the emulsion paint with which it had been painted soon washed off in the rain.

Bear baiting, usually with dogs, was a popular amusement in the 18th century, and this hotel would have been a rendezvous for this spectacle that today seems unbelievably cruel and pointless.

The Weymouth Magistrates Court used to be held in the building opposite the Golden Lion but now their proceedings are held in a different area. Nevertheless, the Golden Lion continues to provide food and drink to visitors and locals.

Overhead, the large golden lion soutant proudly welcomes people into the tavern. For some mysterious reason, the tail of the lion has proved to be a favourite target for local vandals and has needed to be replaced several times over the years.

Weymouth used to have two large successful breweries, namely Devenish and Groves. They merged in 1960 having been considering this since the 1920's. Although they were sited opposite each other, there had always been intense rivalry between the two.

In 1985 Devenish were taken over and then closed down by Inn Leisure Group, a large national pub company. The brewery was closed and the property developed into flats and an arcade – that was the end of a long tradition of brewing good beer in Weymouth.

This statue of a white hart used to stand above the entrance to The White Hart Hotel at the bottom of High East Street, Dorchester.

Although the original hotel had been rebuilt in 1926, it was still very dear to Thomas Hardy enthusiasts. It was mentioned by name in several of his novels and had always been a regular meeting place where farmers and dealers would congregate.

When Hall and Woodhouse, the brewers who owned the White Hart, closed it in 2000 and sold the site to property developers , a furore erupted. The Thomas Hardy Society was afraid that the statue would be destroyed, and another piece of history vandalised.

Luckily, the developers were sympathetic and responded to the pressure by preserving the statue and siting it, with the agreement of the Dorchester Town Council, on a plinth in part of their housing development overlooking the River Frome. So, for once, a happy ending with cooperative developers being sensitive to local feeling.

6

Miscellany

THIS IS THE MEMORIAL to the radar research work carried out at St Aldhelms Head after moving from the Suffolk coast at Bawdsey in the late 1930's.

During this period in Dorset, several major discoveries were made and developed, among which were the rotating aerial that gives a map like display on the screen, as well as the magnetron for producing high intensity very short wave radio energy now found in every microwave oven.

Fearing a reprisal after a 1942 commando raid on the German radar base at Bruneval, the research was moved inland to Malvern. When they left, 2,000 people were working at sites in and around St Aldhelms Head.

These men and women, often working in difficult conditions, deserve to be remembered for their magnificent efforts in helping to keep this country safe and also for the many 'spin-offs' from their work that we unknowingly use in our everyday lives.

The Great Globe at Swanage is one of the largest stone spheres in the world, being 10 feet in diameter and weighing 40 tonnes.

Made of 15 segments of Portland stone held in place by granite dowels, the globe's surface is carved to show the continents of the world and other geographical features. It sits on a ledge carved into the solid rock of the slope below Durlston Castle.

John Burt, as already mentioned, had given much to Swanage, and in 1886 he had Durlston Castle, designed by G.R. Crickmay, built of local stone on the headland south of Swanage. This was really a 'folly' on the grand scale and a place he could entertain visitors to his estate. The Great Globe was carved at Mowlems stone yard in Greenwich and brought to Swanage by sea. From there the 15 pieces of stone were transported to Durlston Point and reassembled by the builder of the castle, W.M. Hardy.

Durlston Castle and Park, including the Great Globe, were acquired by Dorset County Council in 1970 and they are used as a Jurassic Coast educational centre and restaurant. There is a marvellous outlook from the restaurant over the sea along the coast towards The Isle of Wight, and a path and steps lead down to the Great Globe.

This weird sculpture is called Torpedosaur and was created by Andy Kirkby in July 2014. It stands by the 'Park and Ride' on the north side of Weymouth.

Being made entirely of old torpedo parts it illustrates Weymouth's link with manufacturing by the Whitehead torpedo factory, and the Jurassic Coast.

Whiteheads were world famous as designers and makers of torpedoes since 1891, playing a major part in winning the war at sea in both World Wars. Their factory was sited near Ferrybridge so Portland harbour was an ideal testing area for their latest devices. The only evidence of their existence that remains is a stone memorial surrounded by a new housing estate.

The year 1994 marked the 900th anniversary of the Priory Church at Christchurch. One of the ways in which this important anniversary was recognised was by holding a competition to create a sculpture in the Priory Gardens.

The winner of this was Jonathan Sells, the sculptor from Corfe. He had to sculpt a block of Portland stone measuring one metre square by 2.5 metres high that was placed in the gardens and work in situ.

Sells described his design as depicting "…a feeling of rejoicing and celebration with a humorous angle whilst not forgetting the history of the Church". He has succeeded in this by having a different story on each side of the stone, the whole surmounted by the top of the priory tower.

Side A has a monk climbing on the shoulders of another monk to feed birds in a nest; side B sees Ranulf Flambard, who planned the priory and later became Bishop of Durham, marrying a couple; side C has a Norman soldier helping the bishop, signifying the start of the building of the Priory Church, and side D is in the time of Henry VIII and the vicar is threatened with a sword as a monk is kicked, dissolving the monastery at the time of the Reformation. A plaque on the statue gives a more detailed explanation of the carvings.

This work showing the history of the priory makes a wonderful centrepiece to the gardens drawing the eye from every angle, complementing the restful and relaxing atmosphere of the place.

Wenlock, the 2012 Olympic mascot, outside
Weymouth railway station.

De gustibus non est disputandum.*

*Loosely translated: "There's no accounting for taste."

The sculpture on the East Overcliff Drive, Bournemouth, commemorates the Red Arrows pilot Flight Lieutenant Jon Egging who died when his Hawk T1 aircraft crashed near Throop following a display at the Bournemouth Air Festival in 2011.

The five metre high design consists of three glass aircraft soaring into the sky on stainless steel vapour trails with 60 discs in the red white and blue of the Red Arrows display colours. The work was created by Tim Ward of Circling the Square with the original idea coming from children Penny Vallier, 10, and George Cutler, 9, from Kinson Valley Primary School, Bournemouth.

The statue was unveiled at a private ceremony attended by members of the Red Arrows display team as well as the pilot's widow Dr Emma Egging and local dignitaries before the start of the 2012 Bournemouth Air Festival.

Unfortunately, the sculpture is now surrounded by high barriers since the cliff has become slightly unstable. Nevertheless this picture captures the spirit of this permanent memorial to a fine pilot and man.

Sand sculptures have been a feature at Weymouth for over 90 years. The first man to make a living from sculpting with Weymouth sand was Fred Darrington, who started in 1925 and carried on until 1995. His grandson Mark Anderson now carries on the tradition.

Weymouth sand sculptures are made simply from sand and sea water with poster paints added if some colouring is needed. There are no other ingredients except for patience and, of course, skill. The sand on Weymouth beach seems to have special qualities that make it ideal for modelling.

Over the years many different subjects were sculpted in sand by Fred Darrington from The Loch Ness Monster to Leonardo da Vinci's 'The Last Supper' as well as a model of Windsor Castle for a visit by Her Majesty the Queen. Others have tried to compete with the Darrington dynasty but nobody has succeeded in bettering their work.

Index of Statues by Location

Further Reading

If you have enjoyed this volume and are interested in all things Dorset, you will probably like these four other books by Michael Russell Wood:

Dorset's Legacy in Iron and Stone
Dorset's Legacy in Corrugated Iron
Dorset's Legacy in Bridges
Dorset's Legacy in Rural Bus Shelters
Available in good booksellers or direct from the author's website: *www.dorset-legacy.co.uk*